28404693R00061

Made in the USA
Columbia, SC
10 October 2018